Creating Employee Champions

How to Drive Business Success through Sustainability Engagement Training

Joanna M. Sullivan

Founder, Conscience Consulting

jo@conscienceconsult.net

www.conscienceconsult.net

@thinkconscience

Routledge
Taylor & Francis Group

LONDON AND NEW YORK

First published 2014 by Greenleaf Publishing Limited

Published 2017 by Routledge
2 Park Square, Milton Park, Abingdon, Oxon OX14 4RN
711 Third Avenue, New York, NY 10017, USA

*Routledge is an imprint of the Taylor & Francis Group,
an informa business*

ISBN 978-1-910174-15-9 (pbk)

A catalogue record for this title is available from the British Library.

Page design and typesetting by Alison Rayner
Cover by Becky Chilcott

Abstract

DISENGAGED EMPLOYEES COST companies billions in lost productivity and lead to high turnover rates. Yet unleashing an upward spiral of engagement among employees is possible. Making business sustainability part of the job description means employees are driven towards collaboration, community and commitment. And the company will be better positioned to anticipate and adapt to changing market conditions. Sustainability engagement training offers a three-step method for sustainability practitioners to harness the energy of employees behind business sustainability, offering a paradigm shift in thinking about training, employee engagement and business sustainability. Engagement through sustainability values transforms employees into authentic brand ambassadors and companies into movements, so business leaders inspire hearts and minds engagement from employees, foster dynamic commitment to meet sustainability goals and equip employees to engage with stakeholders. Sustainability engagement training provides the tool to achieve a quantum leap towards integrating sustainability into the soul of business.

About the Author

 **JOANNA M. SULLIVAN** is an author, advocate and strategist, specialist in environmental communication and organisational development. For six years Joanna has advised multinational corporations, non-governmental organisations, EU institutions and UN agencies on sustainability communication. Before that, for ten years Joanna worked with two prominent European non-governmental organisations where she designed trailblazing campaigns on public health, consumer affairs, climate change, sustainable economies, agriculture, trade and development issues. She learned how to effect change through people power, pressing companies to green up and policy-makers to clean up. Previously Joanna worked in the European Parliament and the food and beverage industry. Joanna is British, educated at Cardiff, Nice and Open Universities and also speaks French and Spanish. Today she lives between Brussels, Ibiza and her childhood home in Cambridgeshire, one of the first organic farms in rural England.

Contents

Preface

THIS IS MY FIRST BOOK. So many have been swirling around my mind for so many years and this is the first to get written. Why? Because of the urgency for business sustainability.

People are at the heart of every sustainable business. So a quantum leap in sustainability requires people to fully engage in the journey. Wherever you are on the journey of sustainability, this is for you.

I dedicate this book to my children Luc, Jasper and Penelope who inspire me each day to follow the path of purpose in my career. And to my parents Anne and Tony.

And I extend my gratitude to Alison Austin, Nick Bellorini, Rebekah Crawford, Erica Elias, Jeff Halliwell, Hannah Kapff, Katrin Recke, Gaelle Stewart and Katrien Van Eetvelde for such invaluable insights.

Introduction

EVERY BUSINESS has a social responsibility as well as a financial imperative to practice authentic sustainability. Not just to have suppliers, customers and other stakeholders listen, but also to engage in meaningful conversation. To dialogue, ask questions, understand, believe and ultimately advocate sustainability as the path of progress. The days of spin are over. What replaces the old green veneer is a green core around which employees become sustainability ambassadors that can make or break brand reputation. Business today is expected to walk the talk.

Talking in a genuine way about the company, its values and its commitments creates authentic brand communication. No longer top-down, one to many, one-way controlled communication, but authentic communication by employees to suppliers and customers, friends and family, many to many, two-way open conversation at the grassroots. This is why sustainability engagement matters.

Sustainability engagement training can lead to business transformation. Both inside and outside the company, things will feel different. People will feel inspired and committed, able to think with clarity and purpose, and to innovate within the framework of the company's strategic vision.

The sustainability engagement training method enables employees to realise for themselves the meaning and value of sustainability. This innovative training allows people to connect the company values to their own personal values, and the company purpose to their own desire for social contribution. Sustainability pathways provide a mechanism to engage employees for good, through shared values.

Transforming people into sustainability ambassadors for a brand or a business unleashes positive energy, builds commitment and motivates performance far beyond financial incentives. New levels of employee engagement can spread through organic peer-to-peer communication, notably on social media, creating ever wider networks of genuine endorsement.

The book lays out a step-by-step approach to engagement training for business sustainability, transforming employees into sustainability ambassadors, businesses into sustainability leaders and brands into the life and soul of society.

Successful businesses are already taking action to integrate sustainability into their strategic planning. Unilever, Patagonia, Interface and M&S stand out among the giants.[1] And small businesses like Cafédirect, built on social and environmental purpose, are now booming the world over, supported by initiatives such as SEED and Plan B.[2] Sustainability pioneers have set the pace, showing the world a new fair way of doing business. Big companies are playing catch up and urgently need employee engagement tools to transform from inside out.

As the Fairtrade movement empowered consumers to drive social fairness and change, large companies were driven to acquire sustainability credentials. Unilever bought Ben & Jerry's, Cadbury bought Green & Blacks, and Coca-Cola bought Innocent. Nestlé and Mars started to embrace fair trade principles.

Oxfam is nudging the worlds' ten biggest food and beverage companies to go faster through its Behind the Brands campaign to ensure a more sustainable and just food system. Relying on cheap land and labour to produce inexpensive products and huge profits have often come at the cost of the environment and local communities around the world, and have contributed to a food system in crisis. Worldwide more than 1.4 billion people are overweight, and almost 900 million people go to bed hungry each night.[3]

For progressive companies, social responsibility is core to business strategy. Companies are now also starting to integrate sustainability into employee engagement, because companies that do will attract and hold on to talented people. A McKinsey survey reveals 53% of global CEOs believe company performance on sustainability is important to attracting and retaining employees.[4]

Sustainability is good for the *planet*, good for *people* and good for *profit*. This we know. What's less obvious is how to get there. This book is about just that. Through the *parley process*, just like the pirates of former times who had only one chance to find lasting solutions in a space of trust. Sustainability engagement training provides just that opportunity.

....

CHAPTER 1

Putting Social Responsibility at the Heart of Business Strategy: What is a Sustainable Business?

1.1 The big issues: What's driving sustainability?

SEVERAL MAJOR UNPRECEDENTED CHALLENGES are facing business leaders today. Resource scarcity is creating price volatility, climate change is resulting in mass migration, globalisation is forcing radical transparency, and the availability of big data is compelling business leaders to think and act like sustainability champions.

Resource scarcity The world's population is projected to reach more than 9 billion people by 2050. Rising living standards will expand markets for goods and services but place unprecedented demands on the planet's natural resources. Many of the resources once considered renewable – like forests and fresh water – have become finite since human demands are growing more quickly than the ability of the natural world to replenish them. Natural resource shortages will increasingly pose significant risks to the economic and social stability of entire regions. Deforestation, water shortages and energy shortages are all significant challenges.

Price volatility The risk that the world might enter a new era of high and volatile prices over the next two decades is significant. Up to three billion people could join the middle class, boosting demand just when obtaining new resources is difficult and costly. Price shocks from environmental deterioration or climate change will lead to food shortages and price hikes.

Climate change Current estimates suggest that the average global temperature is set to increase by up to 2°C. The impacts will be catastrophic. Extreme weather, rising sea levels, floods and water shortages will impact not just agriculture and fisheries, but also infrastructure and transport. Planning for a policy environment increasingly hostile toward carbon emissions and adapting to climate change require foresight.

Demographic change With explosive population growth in some countries and decline in others, people's goals and aspirations will change. Many of those displaced by climate change will abandon the countryside and become part of the urban sprawl. Half of the world's population now lives in cities. The growing gap between rich and poor will exacerbate social instability. Worker availability, experience and skills will require businesses to fast track knowledge about training, multi-lingual work environments and migration issues. Diversity policies come to the fore.

The global economy The integration of national economies into the global economy has brought substantial opportunities for business, but also significant risks. More and more companies operate in or source from multiple countries with wide differences in environmental and social regulation. Whatever the local practice, stakeholder groups expect companies to respect home standards for social acceptability, human rights, transparency and environmental justice in their business operations globally. Consumers expect their products to be sourced without harm.

Radical transparency Advances in communication technology have reduced not only the time it takes to build a reputation, but also the time it takes to destroy one. It's a world of many-to-many communication, open, uncontrolled, mass media, where everyone has a potential stake in every issue and every business. One quarter of the world population use a smartphone at least monthly, and the same number use Facebook, with 24/7 opportunity for engagement. Twitter counts 240 million monthly active users: 300 billion tweets have been sent since 2006. It's easy for NGOs and individuals to track a company's sustainability performance and to widely disseminate negative opinions. Everyone is a journalist.

Big data Big data's potential impact on sustainability is driven by the desire to understand interactions between business and nature; interactions of business with consumers, suppliers and markets; and nature's own interactions, ecosystems, climate change and lifecycles. Getting a grip of the big picture from big data is now possible due to technology. Business can now understand the impact of their entire value chain, including raw materials, suppliers, customers' product use, how waste is dealt with, and investments. It means having the possibility – or obligation – to take targeted and measurable sustainability action.

According to survey opinion CEOs appear to worry most about resource scarcity, climate change, urbanisation and demographic changes as the top megatrends set to transform business.[5]

Sustainability is driving innovation

People are being forced to think outside the box as the challenges are so overwhelming, demanding thinking and skills way beyond those required of CEOs in the last century. Companies are expected to be profitable, green and socially minded. They are expected to know what's happening at every stage of their supply chain, contribute to the UN development goals, empower women, solve problems of illiteracy, support democracy and civil society and have opinions on human issues of civil rights, gay rights, parenting and education. Companies should sound and act like they have a conscience. Like nothing before, sustainability is driving innovation within business, in communication, energy efficiency, community and employee engagement.

According to the *Harvard Business Review*:[6]

> *We've been studying the sustainability initiatives of 30 large corporations for some time. Our research shows that sustainability is a mother lode of organisational and technological innovations that yield both bottom-line and top-line returns. Becoming environment-friendly lowers costs because companies end up reducing the inputs they use. In addition, the process generates additional revenues from better products or enables companies to create new businesses. In fact, because those are the goals of corporate innovation, we find that smart companies now treat sustainability as innovation's new frontier.*

Sustainability is creating a paradigm shift in business thinking

One significant way companies are starting to innovate for sustainability is by reassessing the economic model in which they operate. Not only are some companies bold enough to report less often than the usual quarterly, thus allowing for longer-term thinking, others are starting to see their operations as circular as opposed to linear.

The circular economy logic is based upon the dramatic reality of resource scarcity, a massive driver to sustainability innovation, and how to make the transition from the traditional linear mode – of production and consumption, inputs in, waste out – to a circular model, based on reusing resources, regenerating natural capital and designing for reuse.

> *The circular economy provides a coherent framework for systems level re-design and as such offers an opportunity to harness innovation and creativity to enable a positive, restorative economy.*[7]

The evolution of the global economy from an increasingly resource-constrained 'take-make-dispose' model towards one that is circular and re-generative by intention poses a huge opportunity for business innovation.

> *Two years ago, we decided to embed circular-economy thinking in our strategic vision and mission, both as a competitive necessity and with the conviction that companies solving the problem of resource constraints will have an advantage. We believe that customers will increasingly consider natural resources in their buying decisions and will give preference to companies that show responsible behavior. . . Designing products and services for a circular economy can also bring savings to a company. The first impression people always have is that it adds costs, but that's not true. We find that it drives breakthrough thinking and can generate superior margins.* PHILIPS CEO, FRANS VAN HOUTEN[8]

Several chief executives in Davos 2014 were keen to show that the circular economy is not just about corporate social responsibility, but about sound business sense. Scarcity of raw materials combined with a rapidly growing global middle class has put enormous pressure on the current linear model of business as usual.

1.2 Defining the pathway: Responsibility or sustainability?

As far back as the mid-1980s the Brundtland Commission's report defined sustainable development as 'development which meets the needs of current generations without compromising the ability of future generations to meet their own needs'.

For the European Commission, corporate social responsibility is 'the responsibility of enterprises for their impacts on society'.

> *To fully meet their social responsibility, enterprises should have in place a process to integrate social, environmental, ethical human rights and consumer concerns into their business operations and core strategy in close collaboration with their stakeholders.*[9]

Sustainability is the solution as framed by governments and NGOs, while corporate social responsibility (CSR) is the business frame. The two terms are interchangeable for the purposes of this book. And the frame is constantly expanding as more is known about the challenges facing humanity, and as technology raises the communications bar.

Increasing circles of responsibility

Companies are today responsible beyond their business success: for their supply chains, biodiversity protection, even reducing social inequity. Many are just starting to digest the big data about their business footprint, and the global challenges facing their business future, developing strategies that can either sustain or adapt the business model to the new realities.

In today's interconnected world, responsible business conduct matters more than ever before. The 2013 Rana Plaza tragedy in Bangladesh demonstrated this. But not only the textile sector, also the extractives, agriculture and finance sectors continue to face major criticism for their perceived lack of global social responsibility. These sectors continue to act in a largely unsustainable way.

Citizens increasingly integrate their own ethics into the sustainability conversation, with animal welfare gaining as much Facebook time as worker welfare, and tax avoidance, bashing big business and brand desecration as popular as human survival. The sustainability landscape is wide open and constantly being redefined. CEOs who don't notice that continue at their peril. It is their employees who know better what sustainability means. It's what they themselves care about and worry about.

Education for sustainability

One of the cross-cutting issues to promote sustainable development is education, highly relevant to business as there is a place for adult education at the workplace. In the Future We Want conclusions of the 2012 Rio20+ Summit, education features prominently:

Full access to quality education at all levels is an essential condition for achieving sustainable development, poverty eradication,

*gender equality and women's empowerment, as well as human
development.*

Education for sustainability is as relevant for school children as it is for
senior management in global corporations, indeed arguably, it is more
urgent for the people making the big decisions today, and those reaching
all corners of the world with business expansion strategies. And education
is also important for employees as a major enabler for behavioural change
to embed social responsibility at every level of a company.

Business has a role to play in education on sustainability

The 2011 OECD Guidelines for Multinational Enterprises consider
sustainability, human rights and education as interconnected.

Enterprises should:[10]

1. Contribute to economic, environmental and social progress with a
   view to achieving sustainable development.

2. Respect the internationally recognised human rights of those
   affected by their activities.

3. Encourage local capacity building through close co-operation with
   the local community [. . .]

4. Encourage human capital formation, in particular by creating
   employment opportunities and facilitating training opportunities
   for employees.

1.3 Leadership in action: What makes a sustainability leader?

Today's business leaders are faced with a myriad of difficult challenges. No longer focused only on profitability, today's executives have to consider strategies to deal with climate change, resource scarcity, price volatility and radical transparency. All demand intelligent and far-sighted strategies. All require thought.

It's especially important that leaders have focus and clarity in making decisions, creative insight to transform their businesses, compassion for their customers and employees, and the courage to do things their own way. Today's leaders think before they act, aware of the consequences, mindful about the future.

Sustainability leaders think first

Try – Sustainability leaders reward innovation and respect failure. They give employees the space to encourage creativity. They let people try and fail, without judgment.

Human – Sustainability leaders act and sound like citizens, not executives. They talk with compassion. They show courage. They are socially responsible.

Influence – Sustainability leaders persuade by the power of argument and not by position alone.

Network – Sustainability leaders build and manage networks, even those outside business norms. In a stakeholder society everyone matters.

Knowledge – Sustainability leaders have an integrated approach to the challenges based on a broad understanding of all business functions.

Facilitate – Sustainability leaders join the dots and create new pathways. They don't think in silos. They encourage cross-departmental conversations.

Instinct – Sustainability leaders are comfortable acting with speed and taking decisions even when only limited information is available. They trust their gut feeling.

Reflect – Sustainability leaders are thoughtful and considered. They think of the consequences of their actions and keep the long-term, big picture in mind.

Storytelling – Sustainability leaders lay out a vision for the business that is compelling, authentic and meaningful.

Trust – Sustainability leaders build it, keep it and don't abuse it. Trust is the foundation of business relationships. Without trust, there's no credibility.

Sustainability leaders stand out from the crowd for their boldness of commitment, inclusive management and integrity. Unilever's well-publicised commitment to sustainability resulted in its CEO Paul Polman being invited in 2012 by United Nations Secretary-General Ban Ki-moon to become a member of the UN High Level Panel of Eminent Persons on the Post-2015 Development Agenda.

We aim to be a trusted corporate citizen wherever we operate in the world, respected for the values and standards by which we behave. We have a set of shared values. Our values guide the way in which we do business and influence the way we think and act. It is by putting these shared values into everyday working practice that we can operate successfully as a company.[11]

Compare the Unilever statement to the words of SEKEM founder Dr Ibrahim Abouleish (**http://www.sekem.com/ibrahim.html**) whose social and environment enterprise in Egypt has become a role model for sustainable development:

This idea of an oasis in the middle of a hostile environment is like an image of the resurrection at dawn, after a long journey through the nightly desert. I saw it in front of me like a model before the actual work in the desert started. And yet in reality I desired even more: I wanted the whole world to develop.[12]

1.4 Shared values: What drives a sustainability champion?

Sustainability leaders demonstrate a combination of masculine and feminine values. That's why women in the C-suite are so relevant in today's business world. Intuition and collaboration are making the business world more human. Once a functional machine, business today has soul.

People aren't interested in how much you know. It's how much you care.[13]

Values reflect how we understand the world, representing our guiding principles and underpinning our motivations, attitudes and actions. When the values of employees are aligned with company values, engagement increases, and the company can make strides towards business sustainability. From shared values, sustainability champions are born. Engaging employees is fundamental to business sustainability.

Engaged employees are the ones most likely to drive innovation, growth and revenue. They are the ones that will collaborate, innovate, build new products and services, generate new ideas and create new customers. They are the ones that will act as brand ambassadors.

Engaged employees ultimately help achieve sustainable progress in the global economy, spurring jobs, human evolution and protection of the natural world. They care because they are engaged in the company's mission.

Personal engagement

Engagement means unleashing the personal power of employees, without which there is little chance to spark the innovative ideas that can address the sustainability challenges. Personal engagement by employees helps develop capacity for joined up thinking and speeds development of the organisation as a whole.

Personal engagement is fundamental to a spirit of innovation, essential to a step change in sustainability progress. Identifying values that spark personal engagement is essential for business sustainability, providing choice, challenge, success, status and pleasure.

Team engagement

Engaging employees through a team lens is traditionally about expecting employees to conform, respect hierarchy and company traditions, but today, the desire to protect people and planet and ensure the wellbeing of others dominates. Values that drive engagement are compassion and responsibility: social and environmental responsibility and concern for colleagues, CEO and local community as humans.

So what do sustainability champions value? From my own experience of interacting with the world's biggest companies for more than 20 years on some of their most challenging public policy issues such as endocrine disrupting chemicals, climate change, public health, human rights and deforestation, to name but a few, the core values of sustainability champions start to emerge.

Core values of sustainability champions

Leadership	Walk the talk
Collaboration	Get down with everyone
Integrity	Be real and respectful
Holistic	Think planet-wide
Transparency	Open hearts and minds
Accountability	Take responsibility yourself
Diversity	Spark new connections

Many of the companies against whom I have campaigned have since evolved into sustainability leaders themselves. Nike today is a recognised sustainability champion, born out of necessity as they were exposed back in the late 1990s as having their products made in factories far away, where they had no oversight and where chemical hazards, social rights abuses and a culture of silence prevailed.

And for all the athletic and cultural and financial successes of the company, I believe our work in sustainable business and innovation has equal potential to shape our legacy. For that to happen, we have to focus on the lessons we've learned:

Transparency is an asset, not a risk. Collaboration enables systemic change.

Every challenge and risk is an opportunity. Design allows you to prototype the future, rather than retrofit the past. To make real change, you have to be a catalyst.
NIKE CEO MARK PARKER IN 2010[14]

And it's not just European and American companies that are making the change. Asian companies are also committing to a sustainable future, such as Indonesian giant Asia Pulp and Paper (APP), which has the ambitious goal of zero deforestation.

In June 2012 we published our 'Sustainability Roadmap Vision 2020'. This was a milestone in our history. It committed us to a journey that places sustainability at the heart of every facet of our operation. This is not an easy path and we are clear about the challenges that lie ahead.[15]

When companies commit to a sustainable future, they need their employees onside.

Ideas to encourage sustainability engagement among employees

Chill out

Time and space for employees at all levels to learn, think and talk about what is happening in the world and how the company can be a force for good in it.

Human to human

Facilitate human-to-human connection, stripping away hierarchy and empowering each individual to self-governance.

Incentives

Make sure employees can account for the social and environmental, as well as the economic, value they create. Make it worthwhile to be a sustainability champion.

Connections

Facilitate cross-departmental interaction. Create opportunities for people to network internally, but also with outside organisations.

Human development

Give people opportunities to develop self-confidence and skills for collaboration, understanding of the business and 'do good' through volunteering or mentoring.

Experimentation

Let people take risks and find a way to test run their ideas and innovations.

Strategies that unite

Involve employees in developing and implementing strategies. Set goals that motivate and inspire.

List developed from Doughty Centre for Corporate Responsibility's seven habits that companies should practice to build successful social intrapreneurism.[16]

1.5 Good governance: Structures to integrate sustainability into strategy

The choice for businesses today is not if, but how, to manage their sustainability strategy. Integrating sustainability into business operations is the way forward.

According to management consultancy McKinsey:

> *Sustainability has long been on the agenda at many businesses, but for decades their environmental, social, and governance activities have been disconnected from core strategy. Many business leaders still take a fragmented, reactive approach to sustainability – launching ad hoc initiatives to promote 'green' credentials, comply with regulatory requirements, or deal with a crisis – rather than treating sustainability as a core business issue.*[17]

For businesses that have been slow to integrate sustainability into their business strategy, it is the exposure to risk that has forced the sustainability agenda into the boardroom. Climate change, scarcity of natural resources, negative publicity over human rights abuses in the supply chain or exposure to litigation over environmental transgressions – these can represent significant risks.

Sustainability leadership advocates CERES believe:

Sustainability begins with board oversight and commitment and follows through into management systems and processes that integrate sustainability into daily decision making. It is this chain of accountability stretching from the boardroom to the factory floor or farm that drives home the importance of achieving truly sustainable business performance.[18]

Sustainability in the C-Suite

Corporate scandals and the economic crisis have heightened demands for new approaches to governance, in part to better manage risk. And as sustainability has risen up the corporate, investor and public policy agendas, it has become more fully integrated into governance expectations. Shareholders, consumers, employees, civil society leaders and policy-makers have demanded greater corporate accountability and transparency, as well as stronger alignment of business ethics with public values.

The key challenge for board members is to establish and oversee stronger corporate alignment with society's expectations while at the same time creating business value. Companies that embrace strong governance for sustainability will be better positioned to foresee and adapt to changing economic, social, environmental and political conditions.

Sustainability training for board members

Requiring board members to have sustainability and corporate responsibility skills in order to be eligible for selection is one way to speed progress to business sustainability. This illustrates commitment to sustainability at the highest levels, and enables the board to provide meaningful oversight for emerging environmental and social issues.

How can board members provide company-wide oversight on issues such as climate change, human rights, sustainable supply chain management, health and safety, as well as sustainable products and services without relevant expertise? Regular education of board members on key sustainability issues becomes essential. Informed board members can help promote a more strategic, long-term approach to the board's overall assessment of business performance.

Management responsibility for driving sustainability

The position of chief sustainability officer (CSO) is not unusual in business today. Several companies have assigned formal responsibility for all angles of sustainability to the CSO who reports directly to the chief executive officer (CEO) and a board-level committee. Progressive companies are thus able to demonstrate that sustainability is a part of all business decisions, from strategy to operations to human resources.

A CSO provides a focal point for ideas, initiatives and encourages interdepartmental cooperation to advance the sustainability agenda and meet specific targets. Importantly, a CSO provides a much-needed interface for the business to take seriously the expectation of stakeholder engagement on sustainability issues.

Yet integrating responsibility throughout a company, rather than limiting it to a single department, raises the profile of sustainability much more among employees. A sustainability council can include executive-level representation from the across the business, including investor relations, communications, human resources, procurement, finance, research, operations and brand marketing, as well as the CEO.

A sustainability council takes a thoughtful, long-term approach to sustainability challenges, discusses risks and opportunities, identifies priorities, monitors progress and recommends policy, and ensures respect for human rights, committing the company to uphold the highest standards for employee health and safety, diversity and inclusion and worker rights.

Employees are often an under-utilised resource in a company's development and implementation of sustainability programmes and strategies. Employees should be aware of a company's sustainability position and goals and should be seen as partners and innovators, proactively nurtured for ideas and feedback. To encourage employee engagement, sustainability must become part of the company's culture, with a clear commitment embraced across the company from the boardroom to the copy room, and through the supply chain.

1.6 Facing the challenges: Sustainability behavioural change

The challenges facing business are, as we have already stated, quite considerable and require sustainability leaders to take the helm. In today's world, only the brave and bold business leaders will survive. Not only are business leaders expected to manage climate change, radical transparency and price volatility, they are also expected to do so under the microscope of the world's tweeters. Overlooking their employees as sustainability champions would be a mistake.

Employees can help a company achieve its business goals faster and more efficiently, when working in synergy behind a mission of sustainability. A shift in thinking is required through sustainability engagement training. Committed, collaborative and community spirited – such a workforce will be capable of operating in the VUCA world as described below, with success.

The concept of a world that is volatile, uncertain, complex, and ambiguous was introduced by the US military as the Cold War ended, as the US looked out over the emergence of a multilateral, rather than a bilateral, global landscape. It's a tool used by Greenpeace among others to prepare global campaign strategies.

The world is complex

Every business situation has multiple interconnections and variables. Some information is known or can be predicted, but its volume and nature is overwhelming. Big data extrapolation needs experts to examine, evaluate and explore possible scenarios, with multi-disciplinary, multi-perspective understanding. Employees must be open, empowered and innovative to drive business strategies.

The world is volatile

Global challenges are unexpected and can last. Will the worst forecasts for climate change happen sooner than predicted? Change is happening at lightening speed so staying ahead of the curve is essential. Being prepared for resource, climate or reputation damage overnight is a must-do. Employees need to work in synergy. All employees, wherever they are based, matter.

The world is ambiguous

Relationships are undefined in today's stakeholder society, where everyone has a stake, and every voice matters. When business leaders reach out to NGO leaders, they are getting into unknown territory. Indeed the idea that business leaders would sit down with their once arch-enemies to discuss common solutions to major global challenges, was unheard of, even a few years ago. With no precedent, new rules are being written. Or progress is made without rules. Human connection as opposed to status is what makes the world tick. Employees need to innovate, learn and share.

The world is uncertain

We may not know what changes will happen and when, but basic trends are clear, at least for climate change, resource scarcity and demographic shifts. Investing in employees, giving them the skills to face uncertainty, the confidence to thrive and find solutions when change is happening all around them, is key. In an uncertain future, the security of working towards a sustainability mission will create engagement.

1.7 Stakeholder engagement: Starts with employee engagement

Facing a world of substantial challenges, where stakeholder society and transparency are the new norms, behaviour and attitude becomes a significant part of the solution. Since everyone is a stakeholder with a voice in business, government, the media and the future, everyone matters to the success of any business.

Stakeholders can be rich or poor, working or unemployed, from the local area or the other side of the world, old or young, informed or completely ignorant. Whatever, their voice matters because it is carried on social media, for the whole world to engage with, or not.

Managing such a diverse range of stakeholders is complicated and risky for companies. No longer will a press release stop the tide of negativity once it starts, no longer is 'no comment' even an option, no longer can the corporate affairs team alone manage the voices that are everywhere all at once, and certainly not from HQ. Local voices matter.

Creating an army of sustainability champions

Since everyone is a stakeholder from anywhere in the world, from any background or position in society, business needs an army of engaged employees advocating their products or services, endorsing their value, passing their messages and diluting negativity with positive stories about the business.

Employees can be this army of authentic brand ambassadors, talking as sustainability champions, acting like they really care, voicing commitment to the company's sustainability mission. They can tell it as it is. What they themselves are doing to help the company reach its sustainability goals. And they can talk when they like, in daily social interactions, not when told to by the PR department. They'll talk because they want to.

> *Our employees turn our vision for SAP into reality – they enable our long-term success as a company and play a critical role in helping us work toward a more sustainable world. Our employees*

are the source of our innovation. They create our products and help our customers run their businesses better. At the same time, they have helped us save energy, reduce our emissions, and use technology to create economic opportunity for people throughout the world. Employee engagement is over 70% at SAP, and is one of four company-wide strategic objectives, in addition to customer success, margin and revenue.[19]

An army of employee champions creates real opportunities for reputation enhancement for companies. So long as they are speaking the truth, unhindered about what the company is doing for sustainability, able to articulate the sustainability targets for energy efficiency, waste reduction, worker rights, women's empowerment, and the progress the company is making towards these goals. It also creates risks to being exposed if business is not all it should be.

For Starbucks CEO Howard Schultz, 'Employees are the true ambassadors of our brand'. The company invested millions in a 'Leadership Lab' designed to train 9,600 store managers on that message. Yet, how many managers would have been able to answer customers' questions about the company's low tax bill in the UK? Sustainability knows no limits.

Gone are the days of heads in the sand. It's OK to be seen as transforming, telling it how it is. It's even OK to be seen as making mistakes so long as lessons are being learned and investments are where they should be. Employees are an invaluable and largely untapped reserve for companies as their public face, their voice to the outside world. In the human-to-human, multi-stakeholder world that business now occupies, every voice matters.

Employee engagement spurs authentic stakeholder engagement

Stakeholder engagement is a critical process that helps companies understand their key environmental and social impacts, identify risks and develop innovative solutions to sustainability challenges. Stakeholders include people or groups within or outside the company who are affected by the company's activities. As we have seen, this can mean everyone. Sustainability engagement training can turn employees into effective and multi-level stakeholder engagement voices.

Employees as brand sustainability ambassadors can help to widen and deepen stakeholder engagement, so while the CEO is having conversations with NGO leaders, the same conversation can be taking place on social media at a different level between employees and their friends.

When Airbus took the step prior to the 2012 Rio20+ Summit to partner with the International Union for the Conservation of Nature on the issue of land degradation, this provided an opportunity for employee education and engagement. Landscape restoration reduces net emissions by increasing carbon storage. The Bonn Challenge, set one year earlier by governments, business and conservation groups to restore 150 million hectares by 2020, became a shared mission for Airbus employees, suppliers and partners.[20]

Sustainability engagement training can reduce the risks of employees miscommunicating about NGO engagement. Effective training is not just about risk reduction, but also about equipping employees, engaging employees and empowering employees to engage with their own circles, family, friends and neighbours on sustainability, as a shared mission.

One of the strongest forces demanding change from business comes from within. Employees and talented candidates today seek work that is meaningful and of demonstrable value to society. They want to work for companies with a clear vision for their contribution to sustainability, and once inside, they look to influence the direction of corporate sustainability and drive improvements through their specific responsibilities.

Employees are businesses' greatest asset. Currently underutilised, overlooked and probably undervalued, transforming them into authentic voices for the company's mission can help cement authentic stakeholder engagement.

....

CHAPTER 2

Empowering Employees to Drive Social Responsibility: What is Sustainability Engagement?

2.1 Driving sustainability: Employees in the driving seat

EMPLOYEE ENGAGEMENT IS A SIGNIFICANT TOOL that can support companies' innovation goals, increase the bottom line and drive sustainability efforts behind the social mission. Sustainability engagement is thus a means to drive a company's corporate responsibility efforts, as well as a goal in itself of employee engagement and the creation of a workforce of authentic brand ambassadors.

Incentivising employees by incorporating sustainability criteria into recruitment policy, employee performance processes and compensation is required. If sustainability is to be more than a talking point then sustainability criteria should be embedded in each employee's goals and job responsibilities, with performance incentives – not just in the incentive plans for senior executives. This can mean, for example, a commitment to reduce CO_2 emissions, source from sustainable suppliers, volunteer in the community or mentor social enterprises.

EMPOWERING EMPLOYEES TO DRIVE SOCIAL RESPONSIBILITY: WHAT IS SUSTAINABILITY ENGAGEMENT?

Oxfam embeds sustainability in the working of all offices by posting monthly data on the energy use, paper use, waste and employee daily transport to work, and recommends tele- or video-conferencing to replace meetings and train travel for journeys up to eight hours. Sustainability engagement becomes part of the team responsibility through raised awareness and shared values.

A number of companies are integrating aspects of sustainability into their human resource recruitment and employee orientation processes. Credible corporate sustainability programmes help companies stand out from the crowd as employers of choice to attract top talent. Companies that reward sustainable job performance, make sustainability a living value for the company. To this end, companies should require that every employee have a sustainability-oriented goal in their annual performance objectives.

General Electric is finding sustainability to be a significant draw for the best and brightest employees. The US company's Ecomagination and Healthymagination programmes help make GE an 'unmatched magnet for talent'.[21]

Just as companies have continuous improvement systems in place to engage workers in identifying and addressing quality issues, companies should have formal systems in place to incentivise and capture employee ideas and feedback on the sustainability vision and goals, and on innovations that will help the company to achieve them.

> According to Cisco, trust in executives appears to have more than twice the impact on engagement that trust in immediate managers does. Executives have to demonstrate consistency in words and actions, communicate often in depth, and align business practices and behaviours throughout the organisation. Engaged employees stay for what they give to the organisation, whereas the disengaged stay for what they get from the organisation.[22]

Motivated employees can transform a business from good to great. When companies empower their employees to think systemically about operations and sustainability, the results are impressive. Ideas and innovations abound.

Empowering employees to think more widely and deeply about sustainability requires a deep level of engagement. They need to care. Once engaged, they will be more likely to stay, as motivated and inspired employees.

2.2 Driving efficiency: Engagement saves money

Employee engagement is a powerful indicator of a company's health and long-term performance. Companies with high levels of employee engagement outperform others. On the other hand, disengaged employees are more likely to leave.

In regions like Asia Pacific where smart young graduates can pick and choose their employer, lack of engagement strategies can be a high price for companies. The Millennials, the generation born after 1980, brought up using digital technology and mass media, are less likely to stay with employers when they don't share the same values.

Surveys paint a bleak picture of employee engagement. Gallup research shows that out of 47,000 employees surveyed worldwide, only 11% were engaged, 62% were not engaged and 27% were actively disengaged. The number of 'actively disengaged workers' continues to be twice the number of engaged employees, defined as emotionally invested in their organisations. Those engaged employees are the ones that work hardest, stay longest and perform best.[23]

Organisations are more profitable when their employees are more engaged. Employees benefit too. Gallup discovered that engagement has a larger effect on employee well-being than all other benefits:

Employees who are engaged are more than three times as likely to be thriving in their overall lives. They are happier, healthier and more interested at work. Engagement is really about what you do every day to make employees feel part of a team. They need to know how they make that team better every day.

What happens if employees are more engaged?

The benefits of employee engagement have been well documented. Employees who feel engaged at work and who can use their strengths in their jobs are more productive and profitable, stay longer, contribute to happier customers and produce higher quality work.

1. **Better business performance**

   - More customer satisfaction

   - Greater revenue growth

   - Quicker delivery to market

   - Stronger financial results

2. **Easy to recruit and retain**

   - More unsolicited applications per employee

   - Lower full-time and part-time employee turnover

3. **Better individual performance**

   BEHAVIOUR

   - Lower stress

   - Less absenteeism

   - Higher productivity

   ATTITUDE

   - Job satisfaction

   - Feeling of value

   - Organisational commitment

   MOTIVATION

   - Consistent quality

   - Higher employee morale

   - Greater preparedness for change

AMBASSADORIAL

- Organisational purpose

- Discretionary effort

- Organisational citizenship

4. **Better team performance**

PERCEPTIONS

- Responsibility

- Autonomy

- Team spirit

- Progress

TRUST

- Openness

- Integrity

- Respect

- Fairness

INTERACTION

- Feedback

- Common purpose

- Reason to connect

- Role expectations

SIGNIFICANCE

- Recognition

- Contribution

- Cohesion

- Innovation

2.3 Driving engagement: Getting employees to care

So how do companies best motivate and engage employees to gain all the benefits described above? While traditional drivers like relationships with boss and peers, career development and company pride remain relevant, one of the strongest engagement drivers is the desire for self-development. Some people seek out companies, bosses, challenges and mentors to help them grow. Others seek the mythical 'healthy balance' between their personal and professional lives. But the real game changer is the higher order desire to derive meaning from work and to feel a sense of belonging. In other words, to be aligned with the company's mission and to belong to the team that accomplishes that mission.[24]

Research from The Conference Board McKinsey suggests engagement drivers are evolving to include a sense of purpose gained through work and alignment with the company mission.[25] If employees' values resonate with their company's values, and if they trust that their company genuinely cares about the same things they care about, then they are more energised and productive. A company's corporate social responsibility effort signals what it cares about. These efforts also appear to significantly increase employee engagement.

AXA Tech launched Rescue-Telecom in 2010 to drive a bottom-up approach to a sustainable corporate responsibility culture. Giving employees the opportunity to volunteer in the Rescue-Telecom NGO providing emergency, portable telecommunication media to connect people within a crisis situation with their families by letting them send a 'message of life' when traditional telecom infrastructure is down, marries employee values with their technical skills. This allows the company to help employees help others. Rescue-Telecom sent five volunteers to the Philippines to support CARE International's humanitarian aid mission during Typhoon Haiyan. AXA Tech's goal is to develop a Rescue-Telecom structure in all regions where the company operates, to enable AXA Tech's employees to help in major crises in tropical and sub-tropical zones where ever CARE is present.

Today's successful companies seek to create a community spirit that mirrors the values and vibe of a movement or a progressive NGO, so people feel they are working collectively for a greater good. With such an altruistic level of commitment, financial incentives become less of a driver, and instead, motivation is derived from bringing meaningful change to society, through collaboration. Work becomes a mission, a pleasure. Employees work in flow.

Yet traditional training continues to centre on self-development. Key skills training develops individuals but too often overlooks the team endeavour. Attention to developing the team spirit makes sense for organisational development and also for sustainable development.

An integrated approach to training should be of high importance to both company human resource departments and to sustainability practitioners. Shared values of sustainability will spur purposeful engagement by employees, boost the bottom line and make work more enjoyable.

If we consider the evolution of human needs,[26] people have an ultimate need for contribution to society, once all other needs have been satisfied. Shared values become real when employees are valued as people rather than human resources.

Figure 1 shows, on the left, Maslow's evolution of needs and, on the right, the typical reward mechanisms offered by companies to their employees.

....

FIGURE 1

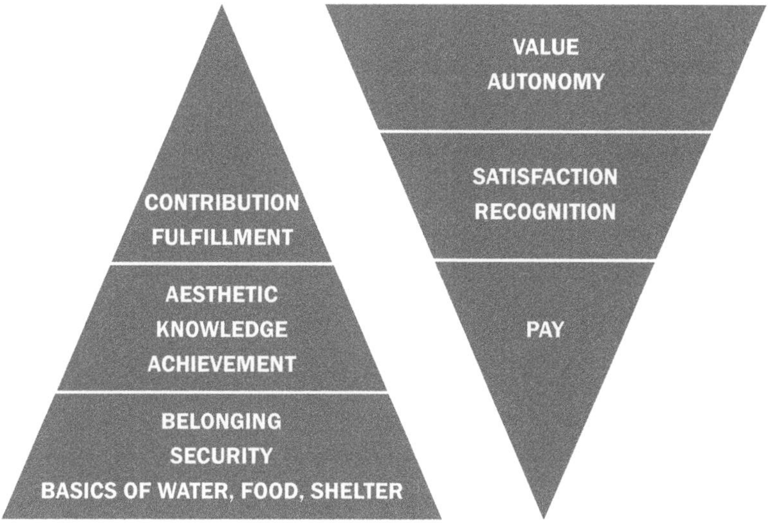

Inspiring a feeling of common purpose and a belief in shared values are cornerstones in corporate evolution. Companies that want to feel, sound and act like social enterprises to attract the best employees, integrate teams and functions, improve motivation and deliver better performance will benefit most from sustainability engagement training.

2.4 Company vision: Engaging employees with the sustainability vision

The advantage of aligning employee values and company values to drive an integrated approach to employee engagement is clear. But now we have accepted the premise it's worth doing, just what kind of vision should companies have for sustainability engagement? Keeping it simple is essential. Something like: the company will make sustainability considerations a core part of recruitment, compensation and training, and will encourage sustainable lifestyle choices.

The commitment of employees will continue to be a critical resource in moving a company towards sustainability – especially if sustainability is going to drive a competitive advantage for the company. Before their commitment towards meeting the company's broader sustainability goals and policies can be counted upon, however, the company will need to demonstrate that employees are themselves respected.

Sustainability begins at home

Where companies demonstrate a firm commitment toward sustainability they benefit from improved recruitment and retention rates, employee morale and productivity, and lower healthcare costs.

Beyond treating its people properly, engaging employees means showing them that sustainability is integrated at the core of the business. Demonstrating such commitment entails embedding sustainability deep into the company culture. That culture begins with each new recruitment decision, and extends to training, performance management and the values that bind the company together as a community.

Since 2008, Intel has linked the variable compensation package of each of its employees, including executives, to the company's achievement of environmental sustainability metrics in three areas: energy efficiency of products, reductions in greenhouse gas emissions and energy use, and improvements in its reputation as an environmental leader. By 2012, Intel had reduced energy use by 8% and GHG emissions by 23%.[27]

2.5 Company strategy: Engaging employees through performance

Employees are a key internal driver of sustainability performance. Efforts to engage internal stakeholders have evolved beyond the appointment of dedicated green teams and internal CSR departments. Now employee engagement is more strategic, focused on core business issues and involving senior executives from different business departments, geographic regions and areas of expertise.

External stakeholders are also getting more attention. Engaging with and responding to external stakeholders helps companies establish credibility and support. It is especially critical for multinational companies to capture the input of stakeholders in specific markets to understand local impacts.

The role and process of stakeholder engagement has evolved over the past few decades. Historically, companies engaged with external stakeholders such as policy-makers to meet regulatory requirements. As companies began to realise the benefits of regular dialogue with stakeholder groups, engagement transitioned into a structured dialogue involving even the most extreme detractors from NGOs and the media. Today a policy of engagement has become the norm, as the value of inclusive debate is understood.

Bringing employees up to speed on the company's sustainability issues will help the process of external engagement. As while companies pursue structured engagement on the big issues with NGOs, informal engagement is taking place every day at the family dinner table, on social media and with friends in social settings.

If employees are not equipped to advocate the sustainability credentials to their local community, in a way they genuinely believe, with stories, anecdotes and facts at their fingertips, then a big opportunity is being missed. Worse the corporate line will sound increasingly hollow if employees cannot walk the corporate talk.

Companies can ask themselves the following questions in order to determine the preparedness of employees to respond to sustainability issues raised about the company and their ability to talk with passion about the company sustainability vision.

Preparedness of employees as sustainability champion:
- Is there an emotional connection to the company? Have you captured their hearts on the sustainability vision?

- Is there an intellectual commitment to the company? Have you engaged their minds on the sustainability strategies?

- Alignment of values. Engaged employees will consistently

> say positive things about the company. They want to tell everyone they meet about the company's vision and values.
>
> - Commitment to the vision. Engaged employees have a long-term commitment to the company. They want to stay to make sure the sustainability strategies are achieved and understand their own role in realising the vision.

Engaged employees will strive to achieve above and beyond what is expected in their daily role. They will become active members of the community to advocate sustainability, and vigorously defend the company against detractors.

2.6 Company mission: Embedding sustainability engagement

It seems logical that the more employees feel the company is actively pursuing worthwhile environmental and social activities, the more they are engaged. They feel commitment to the sustainability vision, motivated to achieve the sustainability vision, trusting of their employers to do the right thing, and loyal to their employers in order to help fulfil the sustainability mission.

Commitment. Commitment means the degree to which individuals associate themselves with the job, the responsibilities and the company vision and values. Engaged employees are those who are committed to overcome every challenge to attain their goals. They are dependable and highly productive and therefore, are accountable for what they do. Their commitment extends into their willingness to advocate the company's values and vision to external stakeholders.

Motivation. Up until recently it was believed that the biggest motivation is achievement. Beyond that, knowledge, aesthetic pleasure, fulfilment and social contribution are also big motivators. But what's clear is that the more we achieve, the more we are motivated. If employees put in a 100% effort to take their organisation to the next level of sustainability, this achievement will motivate them more than anything. Motivation and achievement together act as the ecosystem of any sustainable company.

Trust. High levels of employee engagement are possible only when there is trust. Employees trust companies that are engaged with the future and have a vision for sustainability. Employees must be trusted to experiment to perform their tasks in a different and innovative manner with an entrepreneurial spirit, thinking of the company as a holistic whole, thinking outside of their daily box.

Loyalty. Employees who are actively engaged in their work show loyalty towards the organisation. Recognition is a basic necessity for employees to remain loyal, whether that's through reward or through alignment of personal and company values. The willingness to deliver on long-term sustainability goals means loyalty levels will rise with year-on-year progress achieved.

Culture of open communication

But without an open communication culture, companies will not thrive. Two-way open communication to discuss challenges, potential consequences, vision, values and the company's future is essential.

Training methods should reflect and embed a company culture of open and transparent communication.

Engaged organisations have strong and authentic values, with clear evidence of trust and fairness based on mutual respect, where two-way promises and commitments – between employers and staff – are understood, and are fulfilled. Committing to an intentional culture that's open, transparent and enables employees to thrive is important for retaining top performers.

2.7 Sustainability ambassadors: Employees as sustainability champions

Not every employee is on the front line with the customer, but every employee is still responsible for customer engagement. It is common for behind the scenes staff such as R&D, IT and accounts, for example, to feel disconnected from customers and the public at large. Yet every function is essential to company success and customer satisfaction. Every person has a role to play in speaking for the company, with customers, friends, family and on social media.

Social responsibility drives social media

It's no longer possible for companies to say 'no comment' on the issues they face and any criticisms that crop up. While a select group of people in the company are designated as official spokespersons or given a mandate to blog, comment or tweet on social media on behalf of the company, in reality every staff person has a legitimate interest to comment on social media in the face of criticism against the company.

If employees are allowed and encouraged to experiment with platforms, and they are supported when they speak publicly for the company, in return they will come up with new ideas on how to improve customers' interface with the company.

To maximise the power of such engaged employees, they need the tools and know-how to do a great job of delivering company messages. They must know what the company stands for, its vision, values and mission, know what makes it different from its competitors in the market, understand the brand promise and be able to explain the most important parts of the brand identity, be empowered to talk about the company, equipped with stories, facts and anecdotes.

Sustainability engagement training for employees

Employees can make effective brand ambassadors. They are real people, not official spokespeople, more trusted as they are more authentic. When employees communicate, they represent the brand, giving it meaning and substance. When they communicate on social media they create an authentic echo for the corporate communication.

Sustainability leaders must start the process by engaging their employees and helping them become effective brand ambassadors. Identifying and developing role models of sustainability excellence within the company can be a valuable first step. Employee champions can inspire and encourage others to engage with sustainability.

Training is a key area of essential importance to help transform employees into the embodiment of sustainability values, equipped to communicate and fully engaged in helping the company deliver. The method for integrated sustainability engagement training is described in Chapter 3. Creating employee champions motivates others to become sustainability champions and drives business success.

CHAPTER 3

Giving Employees the Tools to Become Sustainability Advocates: What is Sustainability Engagement Training?

3.1 Defining the method of conscious learning

IT IS ALMOST IMPOSSIBLE FOR A COMPANY to address their major sustainability challenges without also tackling the operational challenge of employee engagement. Embedding sustainability into corporate culture through employee training and support can help engage employees and support sustainability goals.

Sustainability engagement training has major positives for a company. Employees become increasingly passionate about their work within the company and in the community. They are committed and go beyond their role as worker and instead evolve into energised cheerleaders, creative innovators and trusted ambassadors, committed to the company mission.

Training on the broad sustainability challenges facing the company such as climate and energy, diversity and inclusion, and how the company handles specific sustainability issues can help inform, but will not unleash the energy of employees nor provide them with the tools they need to engage.

A more holistic approach is needed that integrates conscious learning techniques, brings employees together from different levels and departments, aiming for employee happiness, empowerment and commitment. The days of show-and-tell training are over. Or at least, it must be recognised that such training serves a limited function of information transfer with a generally low retention rate.

If training is conducted in a way that opens hearts and minds, employees will understand intuitively that they share the values of the company. If the training is conducted in a way that builds confidence and communication skills, employees can be transformed into powerful advocates for brand integrity – authentic sustainability champions. This unique training method is described below.

Conscious learning

At the workplace, formal learning often takes the form of education and skills through modular one-way training programmes. Sustainability engagement training takes a radical new approach. It's about learning from within – a journey of personal power and transformation.

Real learning comes from moments of self-realisation, so participants are encouraged to be mindful and conscious about what they think and feel. Taking people out of their daily thought patterns allows a transformation to self-awareness. This creates the space for values to be embedded.

I suddenly saw my colleagues as people, each doing their best, each caring. I realised I cared about them and the company.
HELEN, 41, FINANCE DEPARTMENT, COMPANY X

Employees connect with one another in an authentic way through conscious learning. They believe what they are saying and believe in what they are doing. They can afterwards talk to others in the same authentic way about sustainability challenges and commitments. The true value of conscious learning is that messages land softly and there is effortless absorption. But beyond that, perceptions, creativity and purposefulness increase.

While conscious learning is about connection, motivation requires simplicity, just like the best NGO campaigns. Training should feel grassroots even though it is organised centrally. People become focused, committed to success. Their emotional fulfilment depends on it! This means total commitment to the company's sustainability goals that will deliver on employee emotional needs.

The 3 Ms of conscious learning

1. **Mindful** – The training philosophy is about individual awareness, so purpose and potential are organic versus taught

2. **Motivated** – Campaigning techniques can be adapted to training to drive commitment to purpose, and motivation to deliver on goals

3. **Memorable** – Learning through activity and play creates excitement, energy and empowerment

Through sustainability engagement training, companies give employees a reason to believe, a reason to connect and a reason to perform. Employees are considered as individuals with their own values and opinions. People understand what they themselves think about sustainability and have the chance to reflect on their own values. And following up with facilitated coaching, mentoring and networks for ongoing sustainability knowledge sharing helps the engagement to deepen.

Traditional coaching is deliberately replaced by self-coaching with the support and facilitation of an external expert. This is not about someone else – a colleague or a boss – telling you how you might think, or how you might improve your performance: it's about learning to think differently yourself as an innovative sustainability thinker.

Sustainability engagement training is the start of a new journey for employees and for the company, the journey of living and breathing a genuinely sustainable future.

3.2 Building the groups for integrated learning

In any organisation, training can benefit all employees at all levels. No longer should we assume that segregation is required, that somehow some employees are smarter than others. No longer should we assume that IT people cannot interface with sales people, that junior accounts people need to be separated from senior executives. There are indeed benefits to all parties to be confronted with those who have other perspectives.

> *I have to admit I had never once stopped to chat to anyone in the pool of secretaries. What an arrogant fool I have been. Overlooking the best ideas.* JOHN, 52, SALES DIRECTOR, COMPANY Y

We have seen by the nature of the challenges facing companies, that it is no longer only the externally faced staff or the media department that have the role of articulating the company vision. All employees are potentially powerful advocates for the brand integrity. All are potential sustainability advocates, with credibility. All staff are thus potential candidates for sustainability engagement training.

Whether you are the CEO of a small or large company, get the sustainability, communication and human resources leaders together to figure out who needs to be trained, in what order and how the training groups are assembled. You may wish to adopt a train-the-trainer approach, so the training can filter through the company more swiftly. High potential champions can be identified in the initial training sessions. They will become the most passionate first-tier employee sustainability champions.

Integrated, multi-level learning

Taking people out of their comfort zones, giving people the opportunity of facing themselves and their attitudes through the eyes of others who think differently and who are trained differently or who have different backgrounds and priorities is a way to open the mind and create new pathways. Giving people the opportunity to interface with people around whom they may be less familiar or less comfortable is a way to free the mind of normal patterns of thinking.

An integrated approach to participant selection helps people to think freely and reach a new level of awareness about sustainability. If employees are emotionally connected to sustainability, they will commit with hearts and minds to working to achieve the company's sustainability goals. Multi-disciplinary groups are the most effective way to build the optimum participant mix for sustainability engagement training.

The 3 Ms of integrated learning

1. Multi-disciplinary training groups with people from different units, teams and departments, within one linguistic group helps create a shift from silo thinking to holistic thinking.

2. Mixed level participants with junior administrators sharing training with senior executives helps create the catalyst for changed thinking patterns.

3. Matching each participant with a 'natural buddy' – from the same unit – helps achieve positive breakthrough energy for all, and avoids isolation.

Advantages of integrated learning

1. **Human-to-human**

   When people have an obligation to explain their own views in a way that everyone will understand, they learn soft skills of empathy and hard skills of articulation. They learn to interact with all types of people that perhaps they are not used to. Since the world today is about human-to-human connection, background and hierarchy become less relevant than attitude.

2. **Value**

   Junior staff and backroom staff feel especially valued as they are being listened to. They have the ear of senior management. By having a voice at the table with management they feel respected, valued and more motivated, which carries through after the training is over.

---

3. **Motivation**

   The expertise in the room will be varied, and this is for a special purpose. Each participant has information, awareness and attitude on sustainability issues that is unique. The people who one imagines to be great teachers are often those we least expect. It is motivation that is ultimately shared.

4. **Integration**

   People get an insight of how it feels working in different areas of the company and how each role is vital for overall sustainability success. People are inspired to collaborate. New networks are seeded. And the company benefits from cross-functional understanding.

5. **Innovation**

   As people consider their own challenges for sustainability within the company goals, ideas start to cross-fertilise between departments, and juniors feel emboldened to share their own ideas. Intense ideas stimulation can result and group-think spurs innovative ideas.

6. **Self-expression**

   Invaluable feedback is gained as people compare and contrast their own working experiences and vent personal frustrations. The space for self-expression in this training method is unique. Non-attributed comment should be collected by the facilitator and given in confidence to HR as useful company-wide feed-in.

7. **Communication**

The obligation to talk in front of colleagues helps improve confidence especially among staff that are not used to speaking their opinions to others on issues outside the scope of their daily tasks. Role play exercises build core communication skills.

3.3 Setting the goals and preparing the process

An integrated approach helps management to be clear what the expected outcomes will be, what skills will be embedded, and what behaviour patterns are expected to emerge among employees. This means in practice creating a training template that is bespoke for the company that can be rolled out company-wide, adapted to local languages, and which has had the input and insight of all parts of the business.

Effective development of the template and sessions requires an external facilitator with expertise in sustainability, psychology and corporate communication.

Sustainability engagement training module development process

1. **Identify the needs.** Undertake training needs analysis to identify the state of knowledge among different kinds and levels of employees in order to effectively target and prioritise.

2. **Decide goals.** Set sustainability engagement training goals that are aligned with the business vision. Sustainability

engagement training cannot take place if there is no integrated sustainability strategy in place in the company.

3. **Determine the approach.** Develop training strategies that meet business imperatives. What emphasis do you want to give the training? What's the big issue? How much time and effort does the company want to dedicate over the medium term? A one-off session may not be enough.

4. **Test the model.** In a key market undertake two or three sessions that provide valuable information about the appropriateness of detail, exercises, timing and venue, so any issues can be ironed out before the company-wide roll-out.

5. **Understand.** Assess results through observation by the facilitator of participants and informal feedback. Review through self-assessment questionnaire the behavioural impacts of the training.

6. **Refine.** Improve the template for the training programme – integrate the lessons learned from the test training and the feedback. Adapt the programme and adopt as the template for the company-wide sustainability engagement training.

7. **Implement.** Roll out the training programme across markets/regions in local language, taking care to embrace and address local issues of sustainability. Get feedback and follow up.

Setting the right goals for engagement

Sustainability engagement is a transformative process with engagement benefits, both internal and external. But before setting goals for sustainability engagement, companies first need to make employee engagement a strategic initiative linked to business value and get the organisational strategy and values clear.

Sustainability engagement training goals

1. **Purpose** – Inspire by articulating the company's higher purpose, the mission that lifts it beyond the purely economic to a social purpose

2. **Happiness** – Focus on psychological needs versus compensation as the primary motivation lever

3. **Connection** – Create community spirit by creating a sense of connectedness

4. **Leadership** – Give participants the opportunity to lead through role play

5. **Communicate** – Give participants a voice, letting them know their opinion matters, the only constraint is integrity

6. **Open mind** – Compel participants to engage with different colleagues, to see other perspectives, to spur an innovation mindset

7. **Sustainability** – Inform on the challenges and the company commitments

---

Getting the goals right took time but so helped orient the training. Just look what we achieved. PASCALE, 46, HUMAN RESOURCES MANAGER, COMPANY Z

Sustainability engagement training expected results

1. Employees are more productive

2. Employees help the company to reach sustainability goals

3. Employees have the tools to engage

4. Employees have the confidence to engage

5. Employees have the will to engage

6. Employees engage with stakeholders on sustainability

7. Employees engage with stakeholders on brand sustainability

---

3.4 Framing the approach to mindful learning

Mindfulness is an essential component of training. Once people feel centred and in the space for reflection, they can consider honestly and openly their own values.

According to the *Harvard Business Review*:

> *The use of mindful practices like meditation, introspection, and journaling are taking hold at such successful enterprises as Google, General Mills, Goldman Sachs, Apple, Medtronic, and Aetna, and contributing to the success of these remarkable organisations.*[28]

In his new book *Focus*, psychologist Dr Daniel Goleman, the father of emotional intelligence (or EQ), provides data that supports the importance of mindfulness in focusing the mind's cognitive abilities, linking them to qualities of the heart like compassion and courage.[29] While neuro-linguistic programming (NLP) is about self-discovery, exploring identity and mission, mindfulness also plays a key role. In NLP terms it might be described as having all senses open.[30]

Sustainability engagement training embraces the three elements of mindfulness.

Meditation. A one-minute silence after each break can help people centre and be ready to learn as well as internalise what has been learnt. Should discussions become heated, a fast way to recover stability within the group is through meditation.

Introspection. At regular moments during the training, people are asked to think, to reflect upon what they know, how they behave, what drives them and what they dream of. All these moments of introspection give people the chance to be themselves and be honest about the way they think and feel. Not only is this deeply therapeutic for some highly stressed staff, it is also valuable for the group dynamic and the realisation that as far as sustainability is concerned, it's a personal commitment as much as a company commitment. Asking people to reflect and emerge ideas themselves is the core to organic learning.

Journaling. At the end of each session, it is useful to have people write down their thoughts and to capture themselves, their realisations. Putting pen to paper engages a physiological creative process that allows people to brainstorm even greater possibilities and solutions to problems. Such a way of transferring ideas, successes and realisations to paper, is a practice that can turn into a regular writing habit. Writing prompts for the group during the training can include:

- What strengths have I noticed in myself?

- What obstacle(s) do I need the most help with?

- What are my core values that motivate me in my work?

- How can I/my business give back to the community?

3.5 Motivating through campaign modelling

Campaign modelling is at the heart of the sustainability engagement method outlined in the table below. Building knowledge, NGO activists gather around a campaign. The more they think, the more strongly they feel.

With employees it works in a similar way, applying campaign techniques to first identify the problems, offer the solution and then provide evidence for change. People move from awareness, interest, to shared values and engagement, and finally to belief in purpose and motivation to succeed.

The motivators of NGO campaigning and employee engagement

What do I know?	Sustainability Challenges	Company Strategy	Company Action
What do I think?	Awareness	Shared values	Belief
How do I feel?	Interest	Engaged	Motivated

Learning preparedness

Open-mind techniques for learning preparedness are required at the start of each training session. Expecting employees to walk into a training session and start to think like activists is impossible.

Energisers compel people to stand, walk, interact, by posting ideas on post-its on the wall, for example, a typical NGO activity to kick off a meeting. Imagination and association are the foundation stones for memory. Combining energy and memory together makes for creativity.

Energiser activities get people in the mood for mental activity. Sitting down all day will not help people learn. To start with, they don't know one another well, or at all, so it's best to dive straight into enforced interaction through playful, yet valuable exercises such as ice breakers. A couple of examples are provided in the useful tools section at the back of this book to open minds at the start of the training sessions.

Once people are relaxed and open-minded, they have laughed a little and helped one another work through some of the exercises, they will be ready to learn. Before we get into the content, just a word on room lay-out. NGOs like to work in a circle facing one another, for their thinking meetings. And for good reason: open communication should be free and unhindered.

Starting by getting people to reflect upon their own values is the start of the journey towards shared values. 'What is sustainability?' or 'What are your values?' can be a good opening question to participants, to start the awareness journey.

Sustainability is personal. So are values. Everyone has a view and everyone implicitly understands global sustainability challenges and values when they are framed in the context of their own personal journey. Both exercises will throw up all the answers there are.

The job of the facilitator is to group the answers into the frame of the company's sustainability strategy. Please refer to the useful tools section at the back of the book for support with grouping sustainability themes.

Learning through interaction

The day-long training sessions generally consist of a series of short presentations followed by an interactive exercise with people working in pre-designed small groups.

During the exercises, communication concepts are introduced, including active listening, story-telling, elevator pitch, key messages, pitch and tone. In this way the playful approach to learning continues through the day.

The journey feels organic, there is mental clarity and people are emotionally connected through the many opportunities for interaction.

The value of integrity

Participants should be very strongly encouraged to always be honest and open about the company's progress towards achieving its sustainability goals. Honesty is always the best policy. Spin is counterproductive to both companies and their employees.

Trust and credibility are immediately lost if mistruths or half truths abound. This is an important message for the training session, and can be repeated in discussions.

3.6 Three-step method:
Challenge, connect, communicate

The three-step method of sustainability engagement is simple, cost-effective and it works! Applying the method can jump-start sustainability progress by big business.

Step 1: Challenge

First the group is asked to identify the sustainability challenges.

Participant-led content

Get participants to think for themselves 'what is sustainability?' Ask them to write three words that come to mind. Tell them they have the answers themselves, there's no right or wrong. Ask them to write key words on big stickers and post on the wall.

Discussion

The facilitator groups the answers into planet, people, profit, parley (the how process). Each person takes it in turns to explain what she/he meant. Get them to challenge one another as to what their ideas mean and what they personally value.

Symbolic map

The facilitator draws a map of the challenge – the people involved, organisations and institutions; and maps out the forces for and against what participants want to happen. The map drawn on the flip chart places the company as a circle at the centre, inside are the employees clearly shown as the most important assets. Key planet, profit and people words are placed around the circle.

Ask participants 'what are your most important values?' Write the key words on big stickers and post on the symbolic map. These are parley process words. They drive 'the how' – the structures, systems and processes for sustainability success. This illustrates the importance of values-based solutions to the challenges.

Discussion

The group discussion provides insights into people's priorities, misunderstandings, concerns and attitudes. In this way, trainer and facilitator get to know the audience. Are they now open-minded? Are the foundations laid for Step 2?

Step 2: Connect

This step provides the core content to participants: company vision, mission and strategy as well as actions that are underway to become more sustainable. It's the toughest part of the session, requiring complete alertness.

Trainer-led content

The trainer, usually the sustainability leader or one of the sustainability team, leads the way. Like any campaign the training needs a red line. It cannot address the 'whole sustainability picture'. Instead it has to focus on a critical path that will connect the participants.

Care is needed not to communicate the full sustainability complexities, however tempting. Information should be delivered within a clear focus on the red line, that is, *the* big sustainability challenge facing the company. Communicate in pictures, not just words.

The trainer should provide their opinion, explain the problem, the solution and the opportunity. Make time for interaction, questions and conversation. Promise to follow up on specifics.

The news

To wholly engage, the training will need to focus on a specific event. Events provide for emotional connection. Talk about a specific 'battle' with NGOs. Illustrate with video. Create drama. And be honest what NGOs think of the company's sustainability record.

Company vision, mission and values

Trainers explain the company vision and mission. The facilitator references the symbolic map from Step 1 to underline the importance of shared values. It's about imbibing a new purpose that will connect the whole company.

Step 3: Communicate

Campaigning is a conversation with society. In the same way the training is a conversation where the trainer can talk, listen, hear, respond and engage with employees, with the support of the facilitator. Having prepared exercises to do with the group matters. Such exercises can help improve communication skills.

Elevator pitch exercise

An exercise whereby small groups of participants write a one-minute 'elevator pitch' presentation about the company and its sustainability mission. Small groups are pre-determined (3–4 people) to allow a mix of talents and experience as well as to balance personality types.

Task: your job is to write a one-minute description of the company, what it does, what it stands for. You will meet someone from outer space in a lift. You have one minute to tell them about the company. The most inexperienced employee in each small group should present the text.

After all groups have presented, there is a discussion on communication, what are key words, how to say them, the importance of appearing genuine, appropriate tone (delivery) as well as language (messages).

Company strategy and action plan

The trainer should explain the new sustainability strategy. Be direct and straightforward. Avoid complexity. The roadmap of actions that the company is committing to should be illustrated with memorable facts, figures and stories. These form the basis of a 'pub quiz' exercise later in the day.

Discussion

Talk about outcomes – who comes out on top, what gets changed, how does it affect people? Campaigning is in essence about a struggle for power. The same applies to sustainability strategies.

Role-play exercise

An exercise whereby small groups write a two-minute presentation about one specific action the company is taking to improve sustainability, and the evidence to back it up, answering the questions: who, why, what, where, when, how much? The facilitator allocates the actions to each group – they reflect the priority actions of the company.

When groups present back to the room, one person takes the role of company spokesperson facing a room of journalists, even though many participants may never have been in such a situation before. The 'journalists' are allowed to ask difficult questions. All participants can attempt to answer.

Key messages
A discussion follows on where key messages of the company are presented, with guidelines for any areas that are off-limits for conversation and communication.

Explaining to my best friend exercise
The elevator pitch exercise can be repeated, as 'telling my best friend about the company's sustainability commitment' using the key messages as the base material, should time permit.

Pub quiz exercise to end the day
Key facts and figures, acronyms and dates can be integrated into the quiz, which ends up animated, as the answers are read out loud at the end.

Ideas to help employees communicate or to help the company be more sustainable can be put into a box in the middle of the training table, so great ideas are not lost.

3.7 Continuous improvement for lasting sustainability engagement

The best time to introduce sustainability engagement training is after change.

- Just after a change of company strategy with a new level of commitment to sustainability. This occurs with a new CEO who is personally committed.

- After the fall-out of a years-long fight with NGOs that eventually compels the company to change direction for the sake of credibility or to keep selling its products.

- After a major change to supply chain management that helps nature and people on the other side of the world, forests, farmers or families.

- After a moment of consolidation, buy-out or merger to align corporate cultures through the glue of sustainability.

Given the constantly shifting sustainability landscape, training should be repeated to update people on content or progress by the company against commitments. Evaluation of people's needs and interests can be gauged after each session.

Some natural sustainability champions will emerge who can be grouped together for more specialist training, whether communications, issue-related, community volunteer activism or coaching. Their enthusiasm to help the company deliver on its sustainability objectives cannot be understated, and should not be overlooked.

They can become training facilitators themselves to speed up implementation of the training programme company-wide. They are the hardcore employee sustainability champions.

Evaluate and improve

Some campaigns fail because campaigners are more concerned with getting 'coverage', than they are in looking for signs of the impact of the campaign. In the same way, facilitators must seek incremental lasting change in behaviour after the training sessions as opposed to relying on feedback forms for measuring success. So what kind of people will the company have after the sustainability engagement training sessions?

Behavioural changes to identify and measure

- More efficient perception of the company vision, mission and values

- Acceptance of the employee's role within that mission

- Spontaneity in behaviour and a more natural relaxed approach

- Problem-centred rather than ego-centred

- Need for detachment to write (journal) or to reflect

- Independent-minded and a sense of personal responsibility

- Freshness in appreciation of the company, its systems and processes

- Having peak flow experiences that can lead to innovations and breakthroughs

- Feelings of connection to others

- Feeling of team spirit

- Attitudes of open-mindedness and open communication

- Capable of distinguishing between means and end, good and bad

- Creativity

- Attitudes and values that are self-owned

Embedding sustainability

This is the start of a journey – a new journey together for employees – so there need to be moments that people can remember when they get back to their day jobs. The end of the training is not the end of sustainability engagement, which can be integrated into company culture in three key ways:

- Skills development through non-hierarchical coaching and mentoring.

- Tools to empower employees to take action at work and outside of work.

- Incentives to encourage people to act in ways that promote sustainability.

What's more, employees will have the confidence to talk to their friends and families, face to face, but also on social media, about the company's sustainability agenda, so will have important feedback to share with employers.

Ensuring staff can follow up the training sessions with a virtual conversation space will provide a much-needed platform for ongoing sustainability engagement.

Final Remarks

I HOPE THIS BOOK HELPS COMPANIES large and small speed progress to sustainability so the hearts and minds of employees and executives are engaged in the sustainability journey.

This book offers the tools and the techniques to inspire, the motivation to lead so competitors have to play catch up, and the facility of thought so everyone in every business can grasp the ideas and implement the three-step method to challenge, connect and communicate with colleagues.

Above all the book is written in a way so it is accessible to non-sustainability practitioners such as human resource leaders, communication managers, managing directors, corporate officers and chief executives.

Creating Employee Champions: How to Drive Business Success through Sustainability Engagement Training is a book that provides a clear rationale for why sustainability in business matters, connects sustainability imperatives and employee engagement challenges, and lays out a proven training methodology that will change companies rapidly into sustainability leaders and their employees into sustainability champions.

I hope you enjoy reading it as much as I enjoyed writing it.

Useful Tools

Who needs training? Sector gaps

SOME SECTORS ARE BETTER AT SUSTAINABILITY than others. The principal reason companies have taken action to integrate sustainability into their business models is pressure from activists: high-speed, one-voice, real-time noise about an issue that is happening on the other side of the world, apparently made worse or actually perpetuated by a well-known household brand.

Today branded goods manufacturers have learnt to embrace change rather than fight it. To accept that being in that privileged place of people's shopping baskets means listening to and sharing people's values. With the shifting perspectives of the Millennials and the empowerment of individuals as protagonists in their own lives, companies, and whole sectors have to listen, adapt and take steps to ensure their operations bring benefits to society as a whole. Otherwise their future is bleak.

How are different business sectors dealing with the sustainability challenge?

Sustainability engagement training is becoming an imperative for the garment sector, since gaps in supply chain compliance leave companies open to criticism for worker rights or human rights abuses.

Sustainability engagement training is fundamental in the retail sector to maintain a motivated workforce, get employees behind sustainability goals, thus enabling some to serve as brand ambassadors to help consumers make sustainable choices.

Consumer goods companies face challenges for healthier products as well as supply chain challenges for resource scarcity. Sustainability engagement training can go hand in hand with a shift to more sustainable products.

Sustainability engagement training in transport companies and the technology sector can help showcase the environmental progress of their R&D departments.

For financial service companies, integrating sustainability metrics into the performance goals of individual employees would be a logical first step.

For the energy sector, a robust sustainability culture embedded company-wide is likely to be a competitive advantage in the future. The same applies to the utilities sector.

Checklist for preparing sustainability engagement training sessions

Get the right support team

1. **Facilitator.** The facilitator is an expert in sustainability and communication who energises the group, reinforces key messages and focuses on outcomes.

2. **Sustainability leader.** The company expert at global, regional or country level used to managing stakeholder relations with NGOs, policy-makers and media.

3. **Technical expert.** The country or issue expert can explain the technical detail. This provides an opportunity for authentic Q&A.

4. **Business leader.** The country managing director can discuss the integration of business goals and sustainability goals.

Get the balance right

1. **Linguistic singularity.** One language only per session, go in-country!

2. **People match.** Balance gender, confidence levels, function, responsibility and baseline awareness (identify groups early on).

3. **Size matters.** Groups of no more than 16 people and no fewer than 10.

4. **Mix right.** Avoid feelings of isolation with at least two people per function.

Get the timing right

1. **One day at a time.** Training sessions should last just one day, ideally off-site.

2. **Regular breaks.** Each module should last no more than 1.5 hours.

3. **Building blocks.** A day of four clearly framed sessions can be expected.

4. **Interaction.** Build in 10 minutes for discussion every 20 minutes.

Optimise the follow up

1. **Recap.** Allow 10 minutes for recap after the morning and afternoon modules so learnings have time and space to sink in.

2. **Tool kit.** Allow 30 minutes at the end to create the dream tool kit for sustainability communication, which can be invaluable for management to understand staff needs.

3. **Feedback.** Allow 15 minutes at the end for participants to fill in a questionnaire as to the quality of the session, how the session could be improved, what knowledge and skills need further improvement in each participant, and other ideas for the company's future. By now it's clear to the staff that sustainability encompasses the future strategy of the company and the company culture.

4. **Follow up.** Create a space for further thoughts and ideas in an online forum which all employees can access, and on which they can post ideas and comments.

Ice breaker exercises

Ice breaker 1

Achieve: Self-reflection, full participation, movement, group reflection & anchoring

The participants are asked to write individually three words on (large) post-its (thick pen) *what they think sustainability means*. Then they get up and stick on the wall their three post-its, under a big sticker called 'Sustainability?'

Together with the facilitator, the participants group the words into four categories – people, planet, profit, parley process – with a core reflection on *how challenging is the goal of 100% sustainability*.

These clusters of post-its remain on the wall throughout the day and can be referred to by the presenters, in the context of company progress to date. And progress yet to be achieved – *the time flow concept.*

Ice breaker 2

Achieve: self-expression, full participation, movement, group reflection and shifting perceptions

Participants are asked to write individually on post-its two words that sum up what they think of the company – how they describe the company to their friends. They are told explicitly there are no right or wrong answers, and they should write what first comes to mind.

Your insights are gold dust to the company. Be honest.

They then are shown the flipchart page that is divided into two columns, entitled: negative (-) and positive (+). Participants are asked to come up one by one and write their words in the correct category.

With the facilitator, participants notice commonalities and differences in opinion. Participants themselves realise that the more they know about the company the more positive their impression is.

During the day, the facilitator (and presenters) can refer to words that are the 'old company' and are no longer relevant, and *focus participants' minds on the 'positives'* that are expanding by the day slowly but surely, as sustainability becomes the new reality 'sustainable company'.

Checklist of business sustainability criteria

  ✓ **Profit.** Innovation and ideas culture that creates and sustains employment

✓ **Profit.** Purchasing decisions that support the development of sustainable economies

✓ **Profit.** Rewarding shareholders for placing their trust in sustainable business models

✓ **Planet.** Efficient use of resources, especially water, cutting waste at all levels

✓ **Planet.** Protecting biodiversity and integrating natural capital into costs

✓ **Planet.** Reducing carbon emissions, investing in renewables and energy efficiencies

✓ **People.** Stakeholder dialogue to promote health, well-being and poverty reduction

✓ **People.** Respect for human rights and gender equity throughout the supply chain

✓ **People.** Employee empowerment through training, mentoring and development

✓ **Parley process.** Sound governance, long-term thinking and inspiring leadership

✓ **Parley process.** Transparent communications so the social value of the business is clear to customers

✓ **Parley process.** Informing and enabling customers in their capacity as active citizens

Checklist of sustainability values

- ✓ Committed

- ✓ Motivated

- ✓ Systems thinker

- ✓ Mediator

- ✓ Collaborator

- ✓ Intuitive

- ✓ Vision rooted in integrity

Checklist of sustainability engagement skills

- ✓ Understanding of new sustainability policies

- ✓ Buy-in to new policies

- ✓ Confident/empowered

- ✓ Positive outlook

- ✓ Open communication

- ✓ Trust in colleagues

- ✓ True team feeling of collaboration

References

1. 2014 Sustainability leaders: A GlobeScan, SustainAbility survey, http://www. globescan.com/expertise/trends/globescan-sustainability-survey.html

2. The SEED initiative supports entrepreneurs for sustainable development: http://www.seedinit.org/. And the B Team initiative works to create a future where the purpose of business is to be a driving force for social, environmental and economic benefit: http://bteam.org/.

3. http://www.oxfam.org/en/grow/campaigns/behind-brands

4. http://www.mckinsey.com/insights/energy_resources_materials/the_ business_of_sustainability_mckinsey_global_survey_results

5. http://www.pwc.com/gx/en/ceo-survey/2014/sustainability-perspective.jhtml

6. http://hbr.org/2009/09/why-sustainability-is-now-the-key-driver-of-innovation/

7. http://www.ellenmacarthurfoundation.org/business/reports

8. http://www.mckinsey.com/insights/sustainability/toward_a_circular_ economy_philips_ceo_frans_van_houten

9. http://ec.europa.eu/enterprise/policies/sustainable-business/files/csr/new- csr/act_en.pdf

10. http://www.oecd.org/daf/inv/mne/48004323.pdf

11. http://www.unilever.com/sustainable-living/ourapproach/values/

12. http://www.sekem.com/susrep13.html

13. Ellis, T. 2010. *The New Pioneers Sustainable Business Success through Social Innovation and Social Entrepreneurship* (Chichester: John Wiley & Sons), p. 172.

14. http://www.nikebiz.com/crreport/content/about/2-1-0-ceo-letter.php

15. http://www.asiapulppaper.com/sustainability

16. Grayson, D. 2013. *Creating Sustainable Businesses through Social Intrapreneurism* (Cranfield: Doughty Centre for Corporate Responsibility), http://www.som.cranfield.ac.uk/som/dinamiccontent/media/OP_Creating%20Sustainable%20Business%20Through%20Social%20Intrapreneurism_March%2013.pdf

17. McKinsey & Company, n.d. *The Business of Sustainability: Putting it into Practice*, http://www.mckinsey.com/insights/energy_resources_materials/the_business_of_sustainability_mckinsey_global_survey_results

18. *The 21st Century Corporation: The CERES Road Map for Sustainability*, http://www.ceres.org/resources/reports/ceres-roadmap-to-sustainability-2010

19. http://archive.sapsustainabilityreport.com/employee-engagement

20. http://www.iucn.org/knowledge/focus/shaking_things_up_in_rio/10109/Bianca-Jagger-IUCN-and-Airbus-launch-campaign-supporting-worlds-largest-forest-land-restoration-initiative

21. Savitz, W. 2012. *Talent, Transformation and the Triple Bottom Line* (San Francisco, CA: Wiley & Sons).

22. http://www.cisco.com/c/en/us/solutions/collaboration/UC_employee_engagement.html

23. *The State of the Global Workplace. A Worldwide Study of Employee Engagement and Wellbeing*, 2010, Gallup Consulting.

24. Ray, R. 2010. Employee engagement in a VUCA world. A review of current research and its implications. Conference Board Research Report.

25. McKinsey & Company, 2012. *The State of Human Capital 2012*, p. 31.

26. Glassman, W. and Hadad, M. 2004. *Approaches to Psychology* (Maidenhead: Open University Press), pp. 278–279.

27. http://newsroom.intel.com/community/intel_newsroom/blog/2012/05/
17/intel-sets-2020-environmental-goals

28. http://blogs.hbr.org/2014/03/developing-mindful-leaders-for-the-c-suite/

29. Goleman, D. 2013. *Focus. The Hidden Driver of Excellence* (New York: HarperCollins).

30. http://www.nlpu.com/NewDesign/NLPU_WhatIsNLP.html

Further Reading

Balestrero, G. and Udo, N. 2014. *Organisational Survival. Profitable Strategies for a Sustainable Future* (New York: International Institute for Learning).

Buzan, T. 2010. *Use Your Head* (London: BBC Active).

Chopra, D. 2009. *The Seven Spiritual Laws of Success* (n.p.: Create Space).

Dennay, D. 2006. *Risk and Society* (London: SAGE).

Jones, D. 2012. *Who Cares Wins: Why Good Business is Better Business* (Harlow: Pearson Education).

Kofman, F. 2006. *Conscious Business: How to Build Value through Values* (Louisville, CO: Sounds True).

PriceWaterhouseCoopers, 2014. *The Keys to Corporate Responsibility Employee Engagement*, **http://www.pwc.com/en_US/us/about-us/corporate-responsibility/assets/pwc-employee-engagement.pdf**

Scharmer, C.O. 2007. *Theory U: Leading from the Future as it Emerges* (Cambridge, MA: Society for Organizational Learning).

Senge, P.M. 2006. *The Fifth Discipline. The Art and Practice of the Learning Organization* (New York: Doubleday).

The Common Cause Handbook: A Guide to Values and Frames for Campaigners, Community Organisers, Civil Servants, Fundraisers, Educators,

Social Entrepreneurs, Activists, Funders, Politicians and Everyone in Between, 2012. (Machynlleth: Public Interest Research Centre).

Tolle, E. 1999. *The Power of Now* (Vancouver: Namaste).

Wilbur, K. 2008. *Integral Life Practice: A 21st Century Blueprint for Physical Health, Emotional Balance, Mental Clarity, and Spiritual Awakening* (Kanhangad, India: Integral Books).

....

Mindfulness for Meditation

MINDFULNESS – cultivating focused awareness on the present moment, developed through practices like meditation and deep breathing – is perhaps our greatest tool when it comes to increasing our capacity for happiness. Take a mental retreat by bringing mindfulness into your day to improve memory and attention, lower stress levels, enhance emotional well-being and sleep quality, and boost creativity and productivity.

1. **Your own happiness is up to you.** Life's happiness, Aurelius said, 'depends upon the quality of your thoughts'. While we cannot control what happens to us, we can control our reactions to the events of our lives, and this gives us strength and freedom. When we ask ourselves the right questions, we gain empowering thoughts.

2. **Life may not give you what you want, but it will give you what you need.** Aurelius accepted that trials and challenges were an unavoidable part of life, but his belief that life and the universe were fundamentally good helped accept the difficulties.

3. **There is good in everyone.** Reach out and communicate with those who disagree, even those who campaign against your company. Aurelius believed that all people are made to cooperate, like the 'rows of the upper and lower teeth'.

4. **True peace comes from within.** Many of us dream of getting away from it all. But, as Aurelius strongly believed, you don't need to

escape your environment to find a sense of calm. We can access serenity any time in our own minds.

5. **Treat life as a friend.** Perhaps the most memorable passage of *Meditations* encourages us to view life as being, in the words of the poet Rumi, 'rigged in [our] favour'. It's a powerful way of reframing any obstacle we encounter.

6. **Maintain a sense of wonder.** Experiencing moments as fresh and exciting, allows them to stick in the brain for longer, becoming part of our lasting emotional memory. Focus on positive experiences with the greatest personal impact. Be present to life's small but joyful moments.

7. **Stay positive.** The longer the brain cells focus, the more of them that focus and the more intensely they focus, the more likely the new thought patterns will embed inner strength, happiness, gratitude and confidence. An essential ingredient of happiness is setting an intention for joy and then insisting upon it.

....

For Product Safety Concerns and Information please contact our EU
representative GPSR@taylorandfrancis.com
Taylor & Francis Verlag GmbH, Kaufingerstraße 24, 80331 München, Germany

www.ingramcontent.com/pod-product-compliance
Ingram Content Group UK Ltd.
Pitfield, Milton Keynes, MK11 3LW, UK
UKHW040928180425
457613UK00011B/301